Clay in the Potter's Hands

Workbook

Second Edition

Clay in the POTTER'S HANDS

Workbook
Second Edition

Diana Pavlac Glyer

Note to Small Group Leaders by Bethany Wagner
Photographs by Adam Bradley
Design by Matthew K. Tyler

Lindale & Assoc.
A Division of TreeHouseStudios

COVER PHOTO AND DESIGN BY MATTHEW K. TYLER

PUBLISHER'S CATALOGING-IN-PUBLICATION DATA

GLYER, DIANA
CLAY IN THE POTTER'S HANDS WORKBOOK SECOND EDITION / DIANA PAVLAC GLYER
NOTE BY BETHANY WAGNER
PHOTOGRAPHS BY ADAM BRADLEY
P. CM.
ISBN: 978-1-937283-10-0

1. SPIRITUAL FORMATION. 2. CHRISTIAN LIFE.
I. TITLE

SECOND EDITION 7 2020
PRINTED IN THE UNITED STATES OF AMERICA

This workbook is dedicated to Brooks, Carly, Griffin, Katie, Peter, Phillip, and Scott, members of The Dante Club, in gratitude for all they have taught me.

CONTENTS

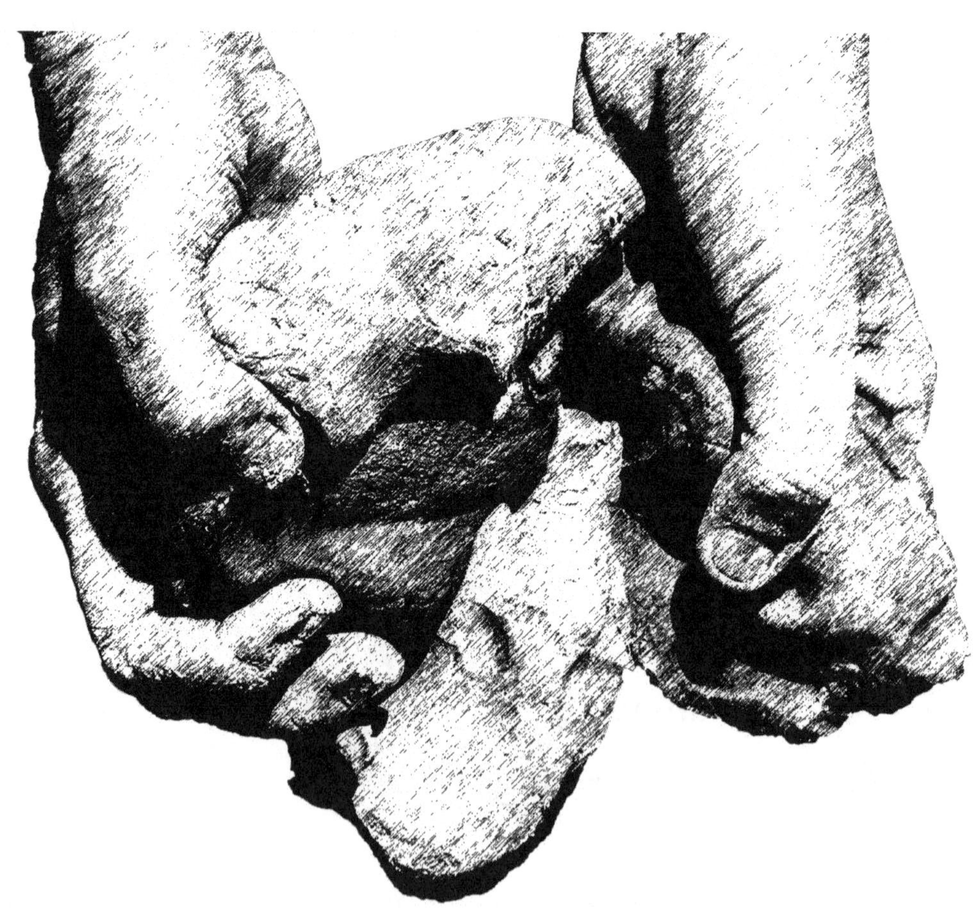

INTRODUCTION

In the Bible, it says that God is like a potter, and we are like clay. This beautiful image has special meaning for me, and I marvel at it every time I go to the ceramics studio, sit at the wheel, and begin my work. It seems to me that the more we know about clay, kilns, wheels, grog, firing, glazing, wedging, and the like, the more this spiritual picture becomes vivid and useful in our daily lives.

In this workbook, I will encourage you to reflect, to think and pray and discuss with others the significance of this transforming image in your own life. These ideas have transforming power. It is my prayer that God will continue to be at work in your life in creative and inspiring ways.

Diana Pavlac Glyer
Glendora, California
February 2019

NOTES TO SMALL GROUP LEADERS

So you have decided to lead a small group study. Congratulations! This is a challenging task, sometimes daunting, but also a richly rewarding one that can transform your own life. There is nothing quite like seeking the Lord in community. Here are some suggestions to consider as you embark on this journey.

ABOUT CLAY IN THE POTTER'S HANDS

Isaiah 64:8 reads, "Yet you, LORD, are our Father. We are the clay, you are the potter; we are all the work of your hand." Throughout Scripture, God is referred to time and time again as a potter. And we are his clay.

This book shows that this is far more than a casual metaphor. As God hovers over his creation, centering us or shaping us or even restoring us from collapse, he may transform us in ways we never imagined. The author guides the reader chapter-by-chapter through the process of creating pottery and illustrates the powerful spiritual truths behind each step.

Clay in the Potter's Hands has been used in home groups, Bible studies, Sunday school classes, Lenten devotions, one-on-one discipleship, and other group settings in churches, homes, and schools. The book itself contains discussion questions and a prayer at the end of each chapter, but this workbook helps groups interact more closely with the text, providing prompts and space for participants to record their own notes, ideas, questions, observations, and prayers.

To go even deeper with further material, leadership suggestions, and additional questions and activities, see the *Clay in the Potter's Hands Leader's Guide*, available at Amazon.com.

ABOUT THIS WORKBOOK

As you will discover throughout this study, God shapes people with care and works in miraculous ways in every life. But this does not mean that every person's spiritual journey will look the same; in fact, like handcrafted pieces of pottery, each is entirely unique.

That's where the workbook comes in, helping participants discover how their stories fit into the narrative of the pottery process and what the image of God as a potter means in their individual lives.

In light of this truth, when studying *Clay in the Potter's Hands*, it is ideal to have time for individual study as well as group study. If your group consists of more than 10 people, some time for discussion and prayer in smaller groups of 3–4 people would also be helpful.

FORMATTING YOUR STUDY

The most straightforward way to complete *Clay in the Potter's Hands* is to meet for weekly sessions, completing one chapter a week for 15 weeks. Allowing 1–1 ½ hours per session is suggested.

That being said, this study is well suited to fit a variety of group sizes and time frames. Depending on the needs of your unique group, you may spend more time on one chapter in particular, or combine two or three chapters during one week. If you are doing a Lenten study, completing 2 chapters each week would fit your timeline well.

But whichever time frame you choose, I suggest having all participants read the chapter, take notes in the workbook, and complete the respective workbook questions and prompts before you meet. Then during your group sessions, you can dive right away into discussing the chapter and your experiences with the text, as well as spending significant time in prayer.

THE 5-SESSION STUDY

Clay in the Potter's Hands also fits well into a 5-session study, as outlined below:

SESSION ONE: INTRODUCTION

This first chapter, "Creating," is the basis for the rest of the book, discussing the nature of God as creator and humanity as his creation. It establishes some key principles that apply to the rest of the book before chapter 2 starts in on the step-by-step process of creating a piece of pottery. In your first session, go through chapter one and discuss how your group wants to learn and grow over the course of your study.

SESSION TWO: PREPARATION

Chapters 2–6 focus on the preparation steps of pottery as the potter finds the clay and prepares it to be shaped on the wheel. These are the necessary steps all pottery must go through before its true shape comes into formation.

SESSION THREE: FORMATION

Chapters 7–11 cover the critical formation steps as the potter guides the clay into its final shape as a pot, cup, bowl, or vase.

SESSION FOUR: COMPLETION

Chapters 12–14 contain the final steps after the clay has been shaped as the potter repairs any damage, re-fires the pottery, and even redeems any shattered pieces.

SESSION FIVE: CONCLUSION

In your last session, wrap up your study with the final chapter, "Abiding." This chapter concludes the long process you have started, and helps participants identify where they are in the pottery process, as well as what next steps they should take as creations of God. Finish with a group prayer for the future work of God in each person's life.

THE WEEKEND STUDY

The 5-week format is also ideal for a weekend retreat or 2–3 day church event. For these more intensive studies, be sure to set aside time for solo study, small group discussion, and instruction as a whole group. I suggest the following structure for a weekend study:

1. Begin each session by introducing the chapter(s) to the entire group. Talk through the potter's steps and the specific actions the potter takes, before moving on to how this illustrates God's creative work forming and shaping us.

2. Break apart for solo time, so each participant can read the material alone, take notes, and answer the workbook questions.

3. Join together again in small groups of 3–4 people to discuss the material, share answers to questions, go through each of the Scriptures in the workbook, and prayer for one another.

4. Come together as a whole group to share any observations as a whole and begin the next session.

SOME FINAL SUGGESTIONS

— Whatever time frame you choose, begin and finish each session with prayer, praising God for his work as Creator and asking him to direct your study.

— Encourage and hold each other accountable to complete the reading and workbook material for each session, and to be honest and authentic with one another as you encounter ways God is shaping and directing you.

— The chapters are short enough that you can read them aloud together. You might read the chapter and then discuss it, or read the next week's reading at the end of each session. Or take turns reading aloud, paragraph by paragraph around the circle.

— Finally, pray regularly for the individuals and spiritual growth of your group. And know that we are praying for you.

May the Lord richly bless you as you begin this journey together!

Bethany Wagner
Portland, Oregon

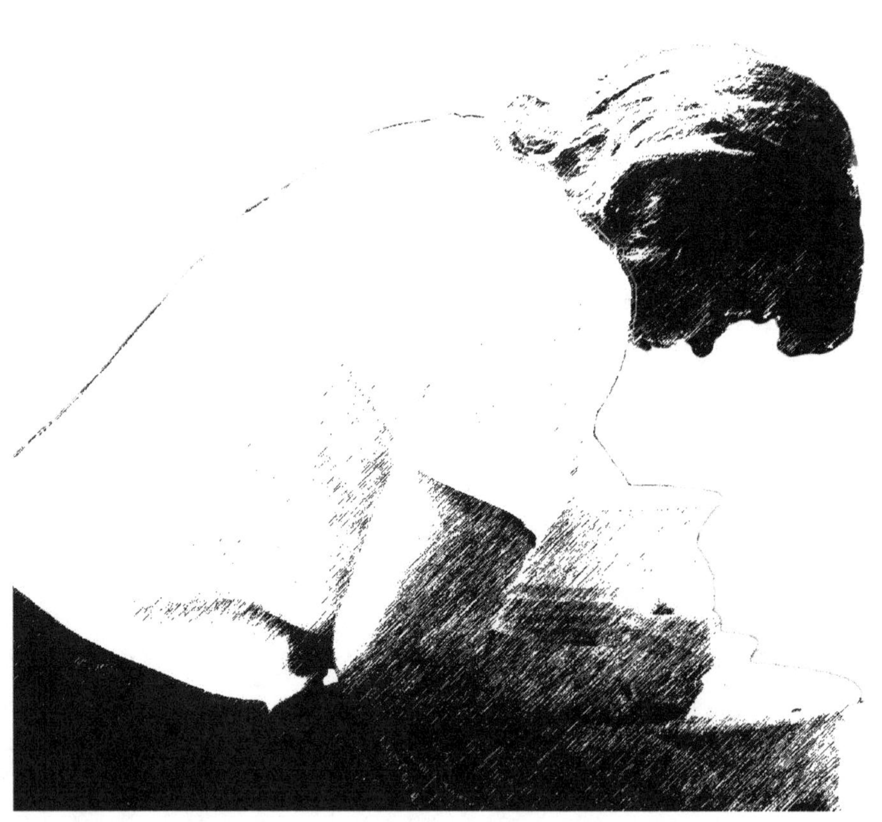

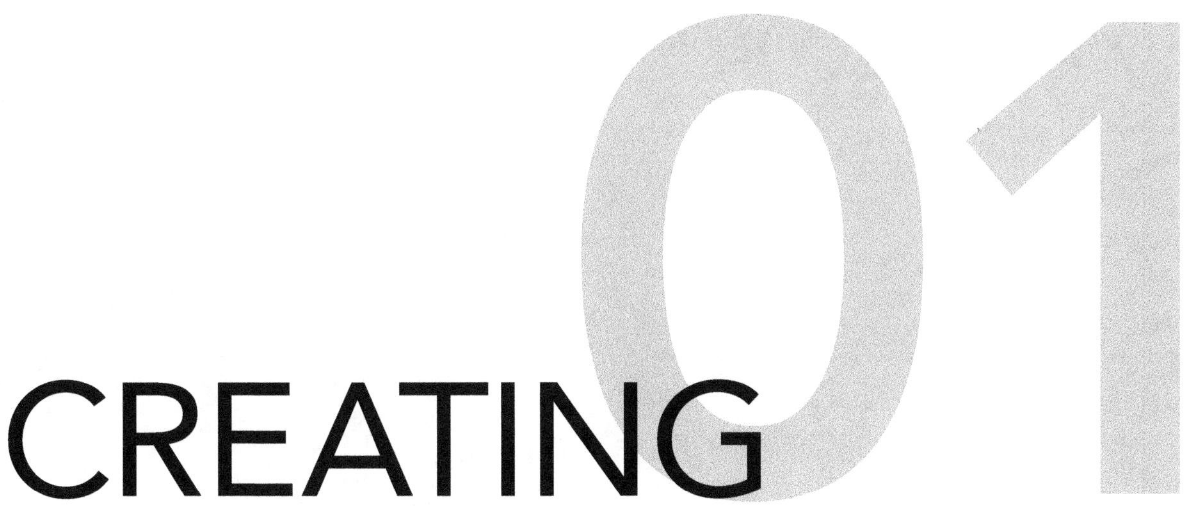

CREATING 01

God tells us that he is like a potter working with clay.

My Reading Notes:

One or two ideas in this chapter that I found new or surprising.

One or two questions that this chapter raised.

One or two places where this chapter spoke to me personally.

QUESTIONS FOR REFLECTION AND DISCUSSION:

1. God is a creator, an artist, a maker. Reflect on a time that you have made things—anything, from rebuilding a carburetor to writing a song to coloring with crayons. What steps did you take to complete the work? What feelings did you have as you progressed from step to step? Did you sense that your creativity was a divine gift, a reflection of the creative nature of God? In what ways?

2. List several times that you have clearly seen the fingerprints of God in the circumstances of your life. Then take time to thank God for it!

AUTHOR'S PRAYER:

You who are the King of all creation have stooped low to care for me. You who oversee all galaxies have become intimately involved in everything that concerns me. You who are the mighty one still bear the marks of your creation on your hands. Open my eyes, God, to see you more clearly in this season of my life than I ever have before. I wait expectantly for fresh insight into who you are, and who I am in you. Amen.

MY PRAYER:

I will not forget you! See, I have engraved you on the palms of my hands; your walls are ever before me.
ISAIAH 49:15-16

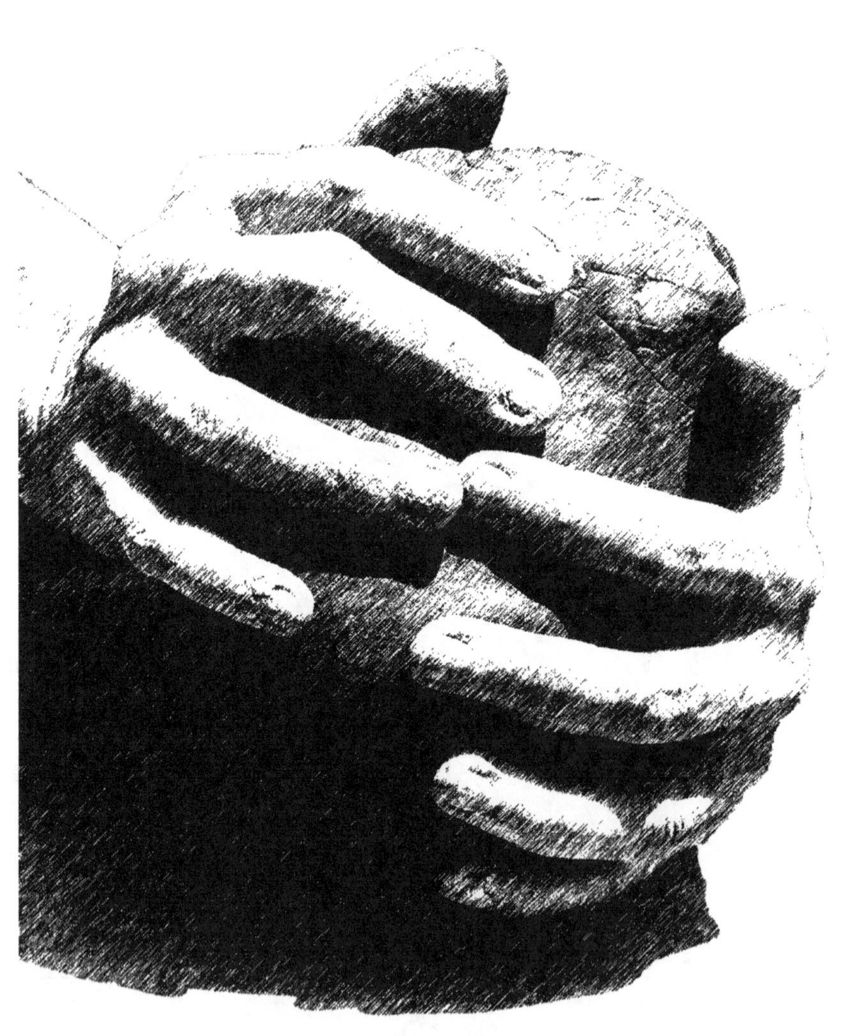

SEARCHING 02

The potter actively seeks the clay and rejoices when it is found.

My Reading Notes:

One or two ideas in this chapter that I found new or surprising.

One or two questions that this chapter raised.

One or two places where this chapter spoke to me personally.

QUESTIONS FOR REFLECTION AND DISCUSSION:

1. God has been seeking you all of your life. If you have responded to his call and been found by him, take time now to thank him for the way he has made you his own. If you have never responded, take time now to consider what it might mean for you, a wandering lamb, to be found and taken home to his fold. Then find someone who can tell you more about the Good Shepherd who loves you.

2. Each type of clay has unique qualities; each of us is unique in personality, abilities, and gifts. Spend some time journaling about the ways in which you are a unique lump of clay. Then ask God to show you how these unique qualities are strengths that he can use.

AUTHOR'S PRAYER:

God, in your goodness, keep seeking after me, bringing me home, drawing me to your side. Thank you that you see in me something of infinite worth. I want to be used by you to do something of great importance. Show me the way to become available so that your miraculous hand can do mighty things on earth through me. Amen.

MY PRAYER:

...indeed, if you call out for insight and cry aloud for understanding, and if you look for it as for silver and search for it as for hidden treasure, then you will understand the fear of the LORD and find the knowledge of God.

PROVERBS 2:3-5

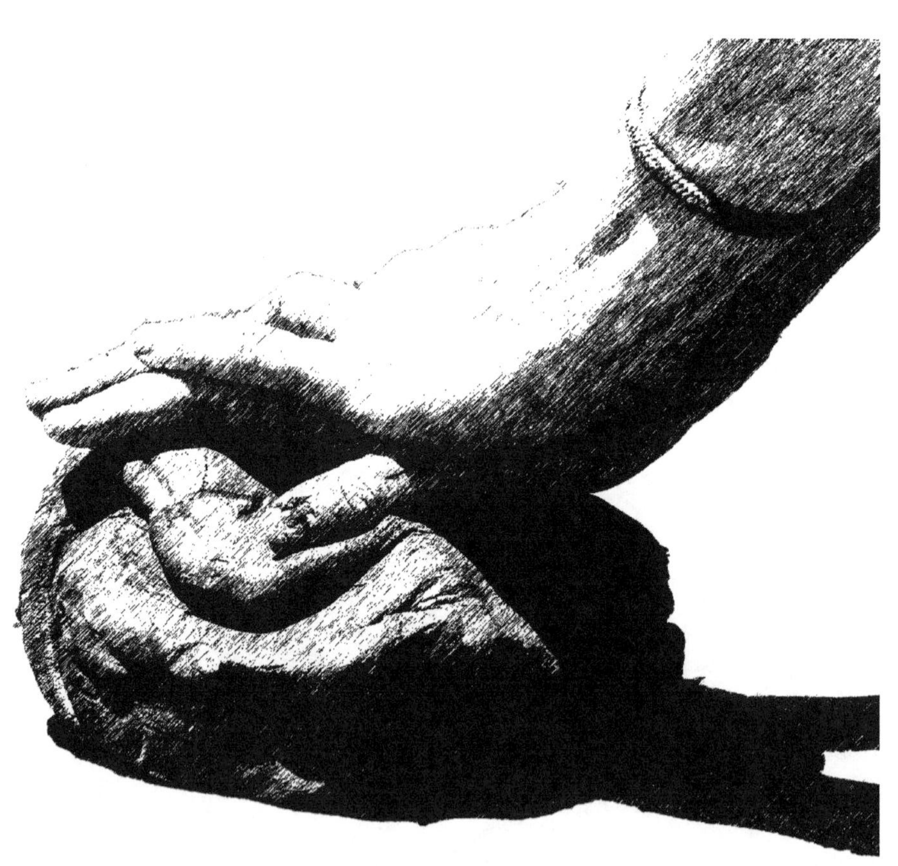

03 PREPARING

The potter pulls the clay out of the earth and cleans and prepares it.

My Reading Notes:

One or two ideas in this chapter that I found new or surprising.

One or two questions that this chapter raised.

One or two places where this chapter spoke to me personally.

QUESTIONS FOR REFLECTION AND DISCUSSION:

1. Are there things in your life, large or small, that God wants to remove from your life because they hurt his heart and injure other people?

2. Are there people you need to talk to in order to settle a matter that has caused stress, tension, shame, or uneasiness?

AUTHOR'S PRAYER:

O God, there are things in my life that I thought were private issues or insignificant matters. But now I see that they really can be dangerous. They hurt me, hurt you, hurt others. I have not dealt with them the way I should. I confess that I've been wrong. Trusting in your goodness, I give you full permission to remove ______________________________ from my life. I surrender it to you, knowing that even small things will pierce your hands. I surrender it to you, convinced that even small things will hurt my sisters and my brothers. Remove the rocks, sticks, stones, and bubbles in my soul, and fill the empty places with healing balm and the presence of your Holy Spirit, in Jesus' name. Let surrender and integrity be my prayer day by day. Amen.

MY PRAYER:

Create in me a pure heart, O God,
and renew a steadfast spirit within me.
Do not cast me from your presence
or take your Holy Spirit from me.
Restore to me the joy of your salvation
and grant me a willing spirit, to sustain me.
PSALM 51:10-12

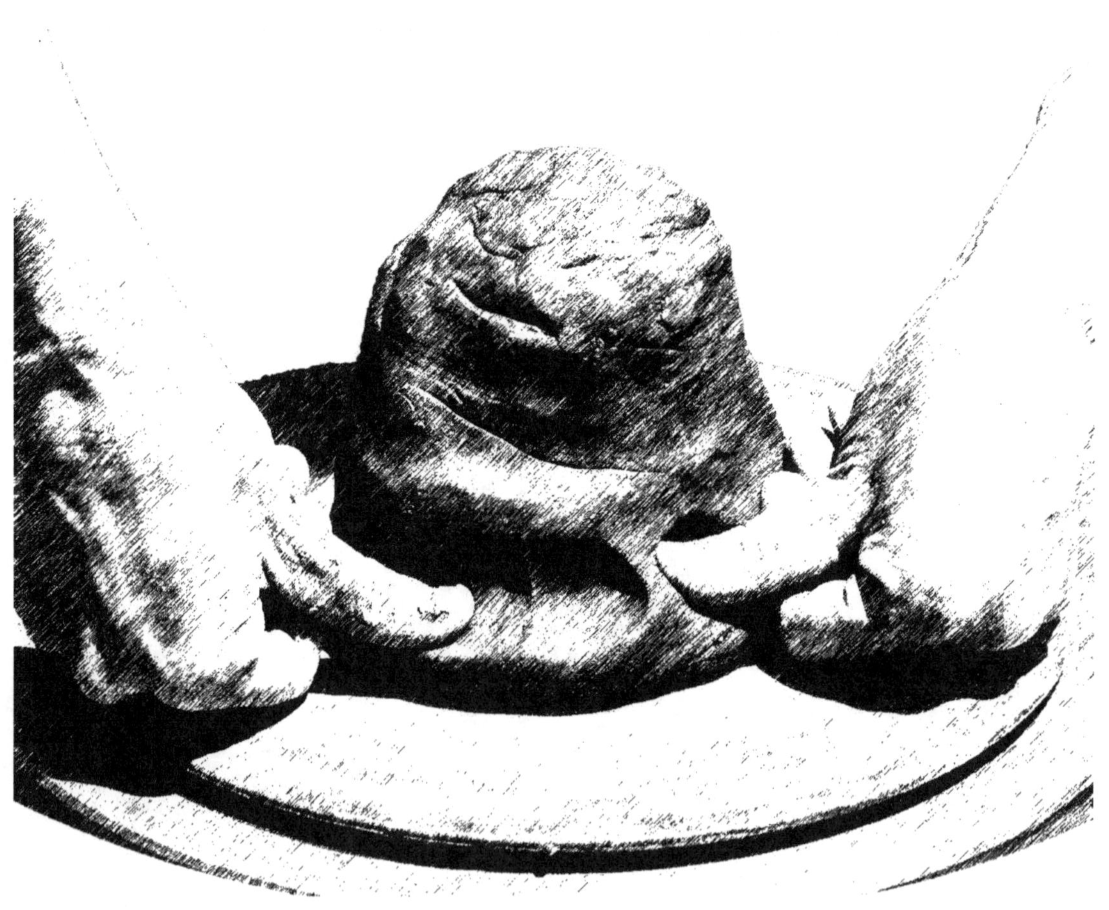

04 COMMITTING

The clay is wedged and then firmly attached to the potter's wheel.

My Reading Notes:

One or two ideas in this chapter that I found new or surprising.

One or two questions that this chapter raised.

One or two places where this chapter spoke to me personally.

QUESTIONS FOR REFLECTION AND DISCUSSION:

1. Has God convinced you of any area of your life that is not going well because you haven't made a decisive commitment? If so, take time to make that commitment sure.

2. Think about the long-term projects that you are in the midst of. List them. Then ask for God's help to strengthen your resolve and help you finish well.

AUTHOR'S PRAYER:

Forgive me, Gracious Heavenly Father, for the times I have broken my commitments because the situation just got too hard. Show me if I need to take steps to repair any damage I have caused. And now, rekindle hope in my heart to face the challenges that are before me this day. Give me the strength and courage to persevere in those things that you have called me to do. And when I come to the end of my life, let me say with the Apostle Paul, "I have fought the good fight, I have finished the race, I have kept the faith" (2 Timothy 4:7). Then let me run the race, this day, with cheerful endurance. Amen.

MY PRAYER:

Do you not know that in a race all the runners run, but only one gets the prize? Run in such a way as to get the prize. Everyone who competes in the games goes into strict training. They do it to get a crown that will not last, but we do it to get a crown that will last forever.

1 CORINTHIANS 9:24-25

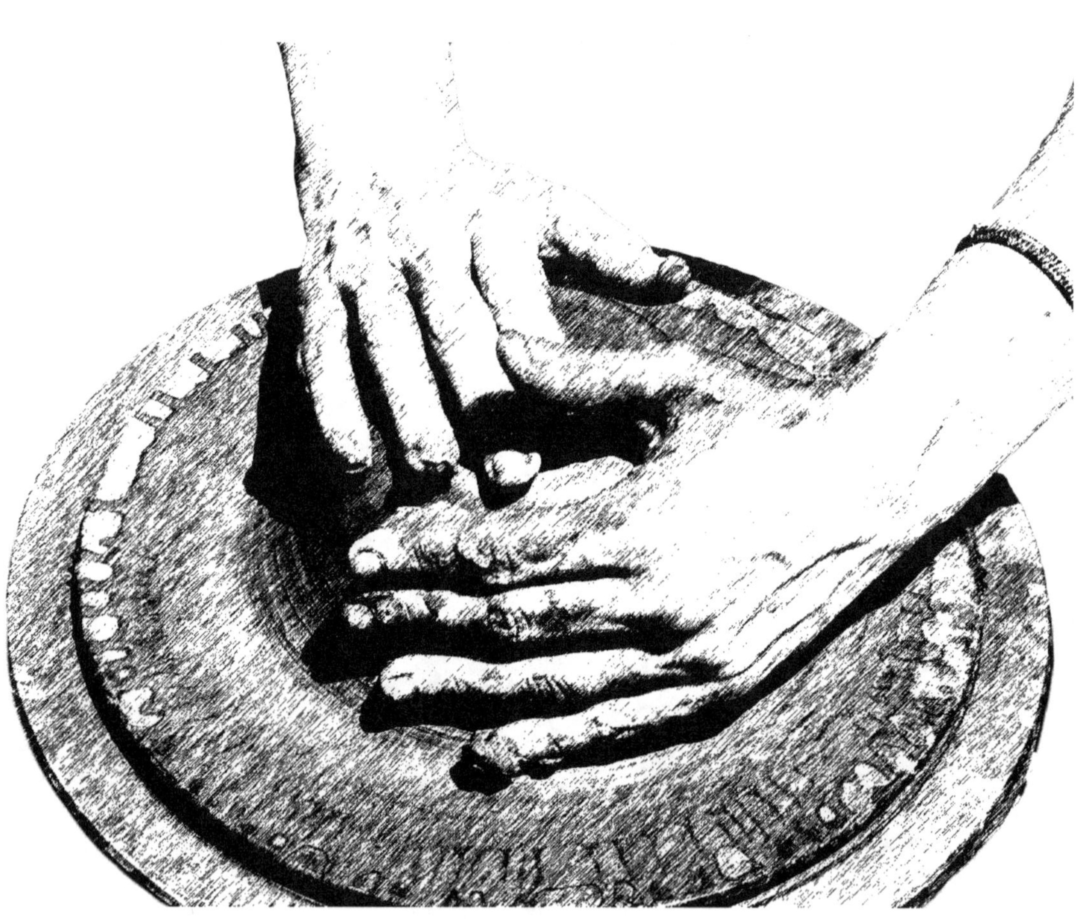

05 CENTERING

*The potter spins the potter's wheel,
applies water, and centers the clay.*

My Reading Notes:

One or two ideas in this chapter that I found new or surprising.

One or two questions that this chapter raised.

One or two places where this chapter spoke to me personally.

QUESTIONS FOR REFLECTION AND DISCUSSION:

1. Reflect on your schedule this past week. Was it characterized by joy and peace, ease and strength? Or was it marred by fearful striving? Were you able to find moments of Shalom despite the push and pull of life's circumstances?

2. Now get specific: What changes do you need to make in your life so that the Great Shalom, the peace of God, is an ever-increasing part of your daily life?

AUTHOR'S PRAYER:

Lord God, I don't want to be tossed to and fro by the screeching demands of my circumstances. I want to rest under your hand, quiet, content, strong, and centered. Rather than trying harder to fix all this, I choose to slow down, breathe deep, open my hands, and let it go. Amen.

MY PRAYER:

...being confident of this, that he who began a good work in you will carry it on to completion until the day of Christ Jesus.
PHILIPPIANS 1:6

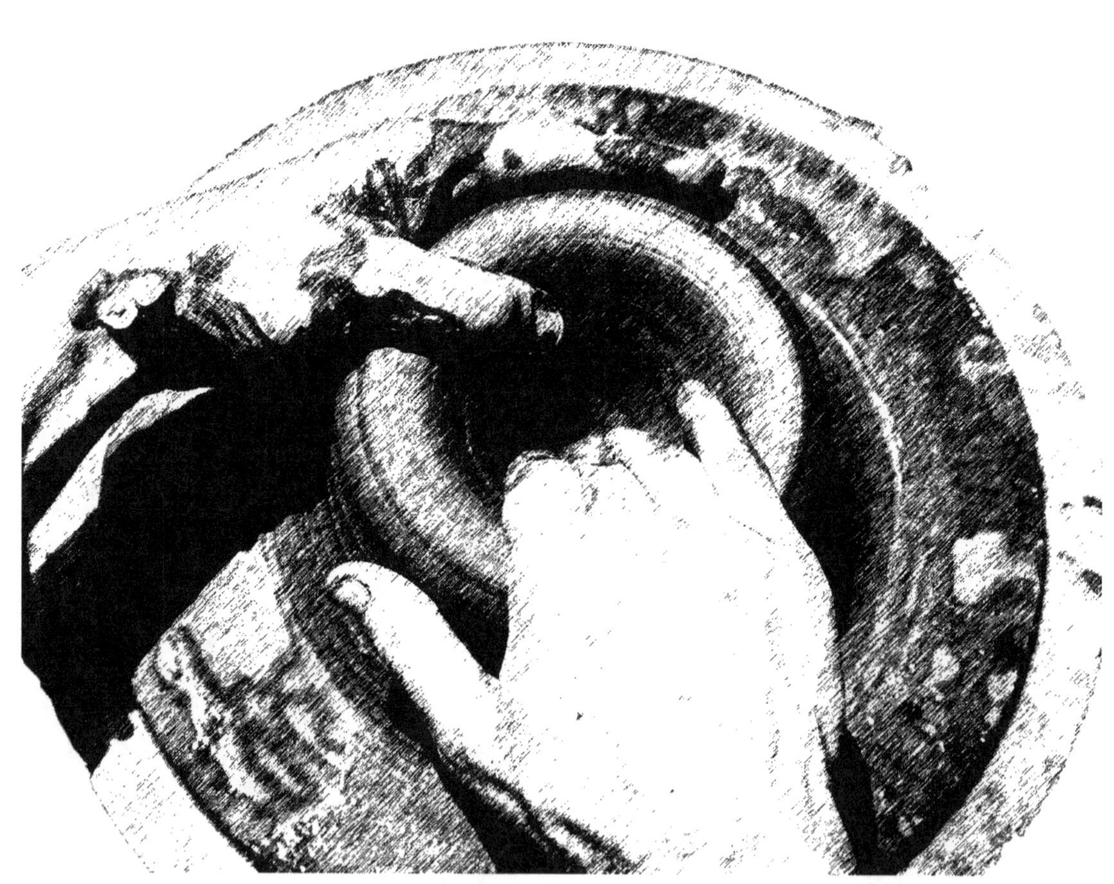

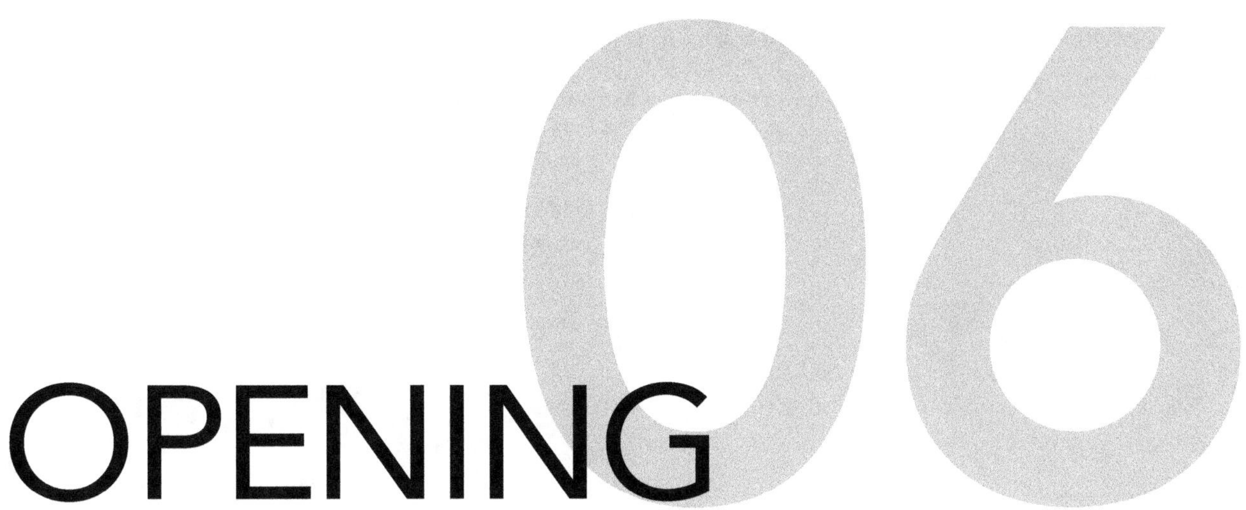

OPENING 06

The potter presses into the center and opens the clay.

My Reading Notes:

One or two ideas in this chapter that I found new or surprising.

One or two questions that this chapter raised.

One or two places where this chapter spoke to me personally.

QUESTIONS FOR REFLECTION AND DISCUSSION:

1. To what extent have you filled up your schedule and your heart as a way of avoiding the scary feeling of being empty? Can you identify any specific things that you need to push out of the way in order to make room for the whisper of God?

2. Search your heart and then your calendar: Can you make specific time for solitude, silence, fasting, and/or releasing sometime in the next month?

AUTHOR'S PRAYER:

God, it is true—I am better at hanging on to things than letting them go. As a result, my life has gotten so crowded that there is little room for the new things that you want to pour into my life. To be honest, there really isn't very much room for you, either. I don't like to admit it, but I am an awful lot like that innkeeper in Bethlehem who crammed his place full to overflowing, and when the King of Glory came to call, there was no room. Forgive my self-indulgence. Heal my fears. And teach me to be available and open to you. Amen.

MY PRAYER:

The Lord said, "Go out and stand on the mountain in the presence of the Lord, for the Lord is about to pass by." Then a great and powerful wind tore the mountains apart and shattered the rocks before the Lord, but the Lord was not in the wind. After the wind there was an earthquake, but the Lord was not in the earthquake. After the earthquake came a fire, but the Lord was not in the fire. And after the fire came a gentle whisper.

1 KINGS 19:11-12

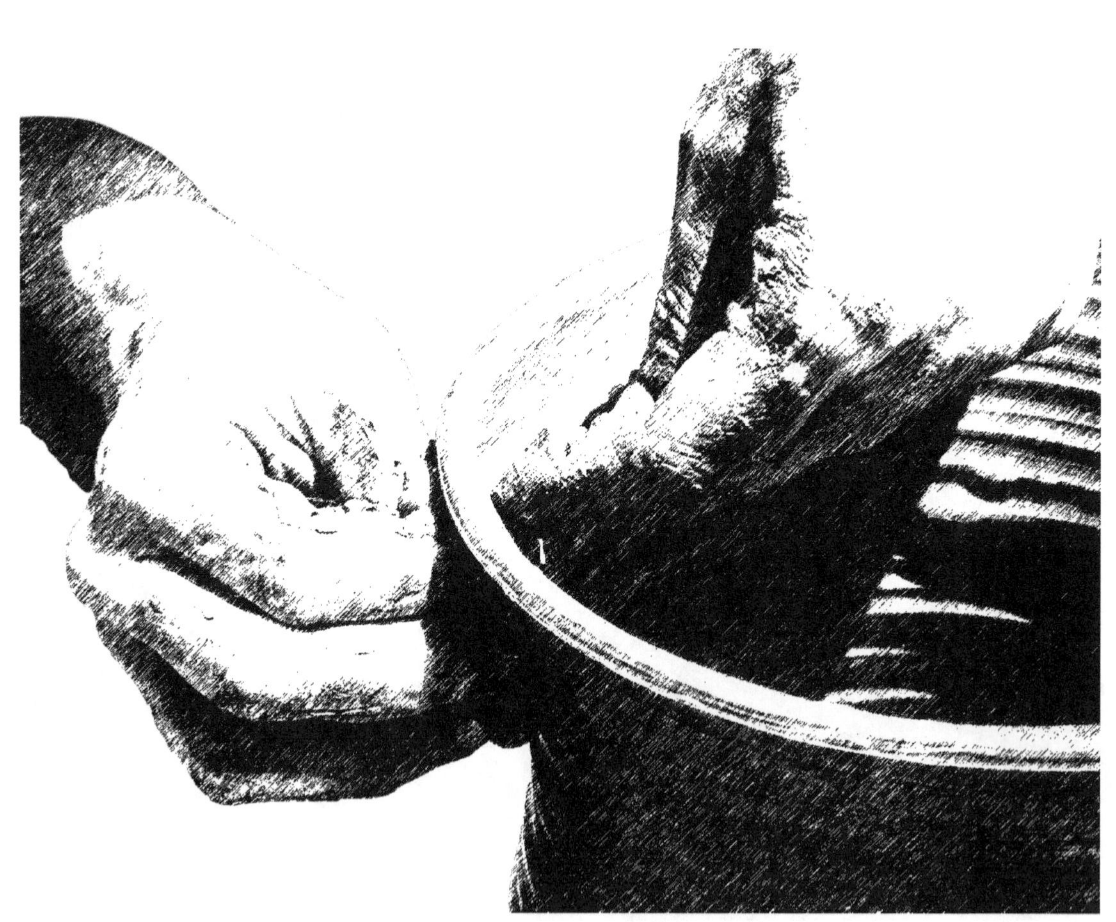

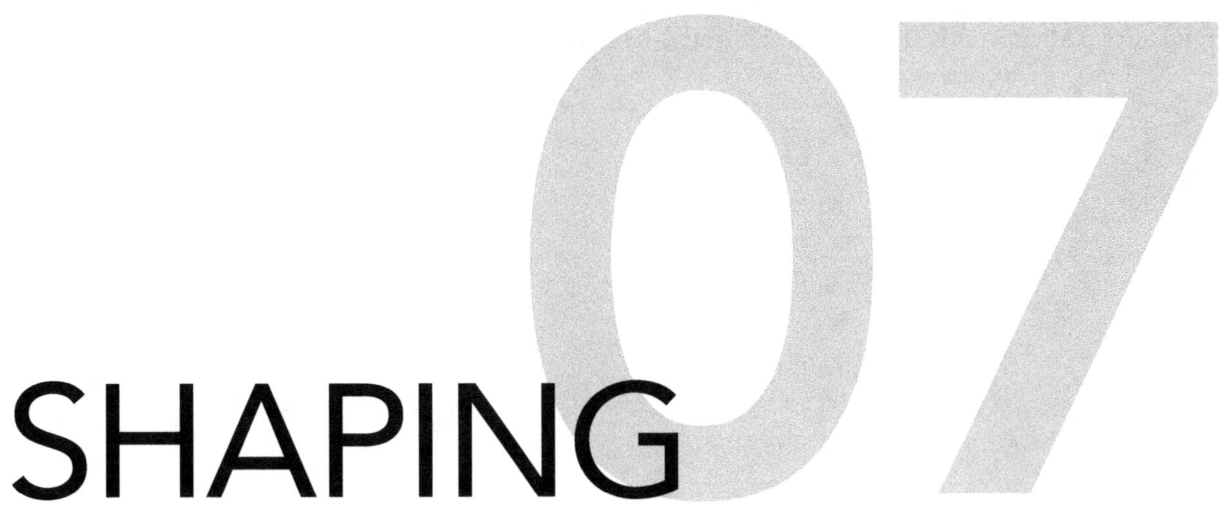

07 SHAPING

The potter uses pressure, inside and out, to shape the clay.

My Reading Notes:

One or two ideas in this chapter that I found new or surprising.

One or two questions that this chapter raised.

One or two places where this chapter spoke to me personally.

QUESTIONS FOR REFLECTION AND DISCUSSION:

1. Think about the shape of your past. Is there an unexpected turn of events that didn't make sense at the time, but now is a clear indication of God's good and perfect will? Share that story with someone this week. It will be an encouragement to them and to you.

2. Think about the shape of your future. In your heart, are you clear about saying an unconditional "Yes!" to Jesus, the Lord? If you sense a place of resistance, ask for God's help to identify it and understand it and work through it.

AUTHOR'S PRAYER:

Lord, forgive me for all of the times that I have argued, explained, excused, and fought the shaping process in my life. I really do want the shape of my life to reflect your good and perfect will. I really want the shape of my soul to reflect the character and nature of Jesus.

Sometimes I'm not very good at saying yes, Lord. But I want to get better at it. So let me make this declaration now. If you want to make my life into something that is useful to your kingdom, take me. I've said no, maybe, later, we'll see. Today I say, "Yes, Lord."

And tomorrow when I wake, pour out a fresh batch of grace so that I have all that I need to say, "Yes, Lord" again.

Thank you for loving me enough to keep forming and shaping and molding and working in my life, day by day by day. Amen.

MY PRAYER:

Then I heard the voice of the Lord saying, "Whom shall I send? And who will go for us?" And I said, "Here am I. Send me!"

ISAIAH 6:8

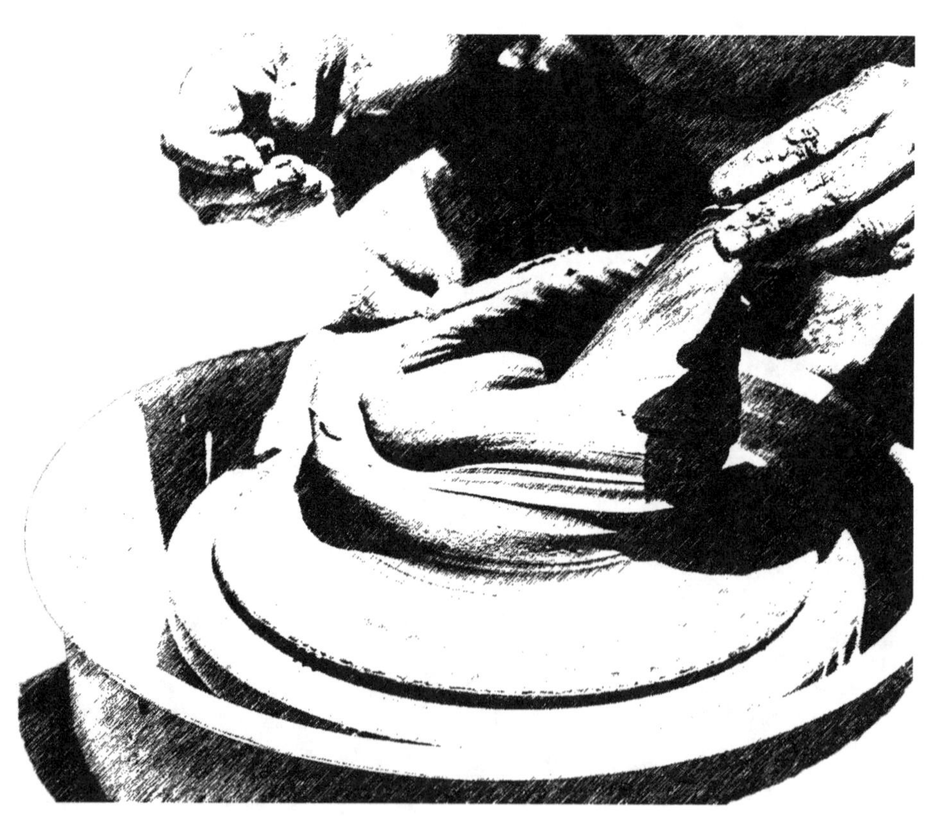

08 RESTORING

*If the clay pot weakens, wobbles,
and collapses, God is not daunted.*

My Reading Notes:

One or two ideas in this chapter that I found new or surprising.

One or two questions that this chapter raised.

One or two places where this chapter spoke to me personally.

QUESTIONS FOR REFLECTION AND DISCUSSION:

1. Fatigue is a fact of life for most of us. Consider if there is a need in your life right now to make changes that will bring refreshment and prevent the destruction to mind and body that comes from accumulated fatigue. Then consider: Is someone you know facing serious challenges in the push and pull of life? Is there something you (or your small group) can do this week to reduce the stress and help carry the load?

2. Think of a time when you have faced a major setback—when things did not go smoothly, when the process was interrupted with an unexpected collapse. Do you have a testimony of the way that God can move into a situation, and start all over again?

AUTHOR'S PRAYER:

Identify one particular situation that seems beyond repair.

Then pray:

Lord, I just can't see how this mess could possibly be made right. Give me the strength to scoop up this whole situation, every bit of it, put it in your loving hands, and trust you to make it right again. Amen.

MY PRAYER:

Do you not know? Have you not heard? The LORD is the everlasting God, the Creator of the ends of the earth. He will not grow tired or weary, and his understanding no one can fathom. He gives strength to the weary and increases the power of the weak. Even youths grow tired and weary, and young men stumble and fall; but those who hope in the LORD will renew their strength. They will soar on wings like eagles; they will run and not grow weary, they will walk and not be faint.

ISAIAH 40:28-31

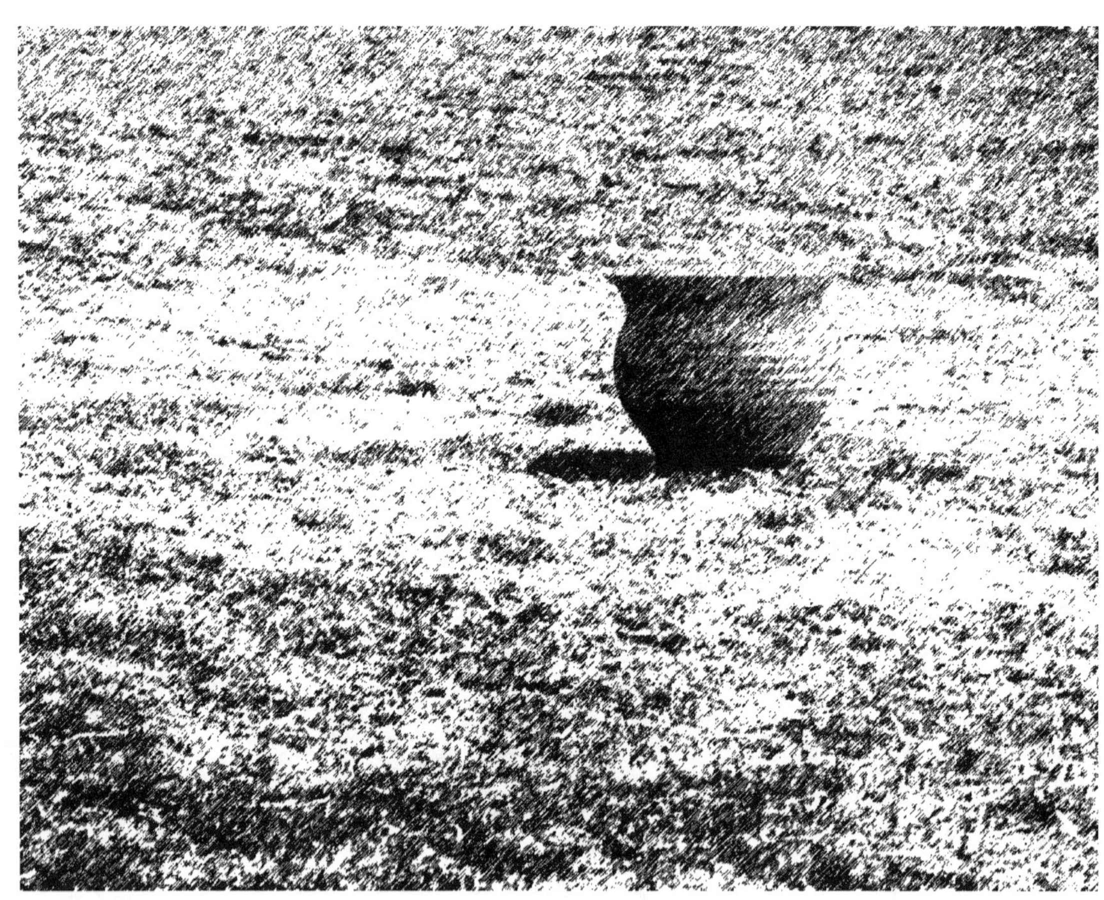

09 PERSISTING

The pot is taken off the wheel and left to dry.

My Reading Notes:

One or two ideas in this chapter that I found new or surprising.

One or two questions that this chapter raised.

One or two places where this chapter spoke to me personally.

QUESTIONS FOR REFLECTION AND DISCUSSION:

1. Is there a time in your life when a project has been ruined or compromised because you were impatient and skipped some steps along the way? Ask God to forgive you, and then ask him to show you what you might learn from the experience.

2. Is there a particular project or event or issue in your life right now that seems to be on hold? Find someone to pray with this week and seek God's direction concerning it. With the help of a trusted friend, seek to discern if now is the time for things to change, or if this is a time to wait. Patiently. For the fullness of time. Until this stage of the process is truly completed.

AUTHOR'S PRAYER:

God, I do not like to wait. I don't really trust the dry times when nothing seems to be happening. Help me to grow in trust and patience so that I can understand what John Milton meant when he wrote, "They also serve who only stand and wait." Amen.

MY PRAYER:

I remain confident of this: I will see the goodness of the LORD in the land of the living. Wait for the LORD; be strong and take heart and wait for the LORD.
PSALM 27:13-14

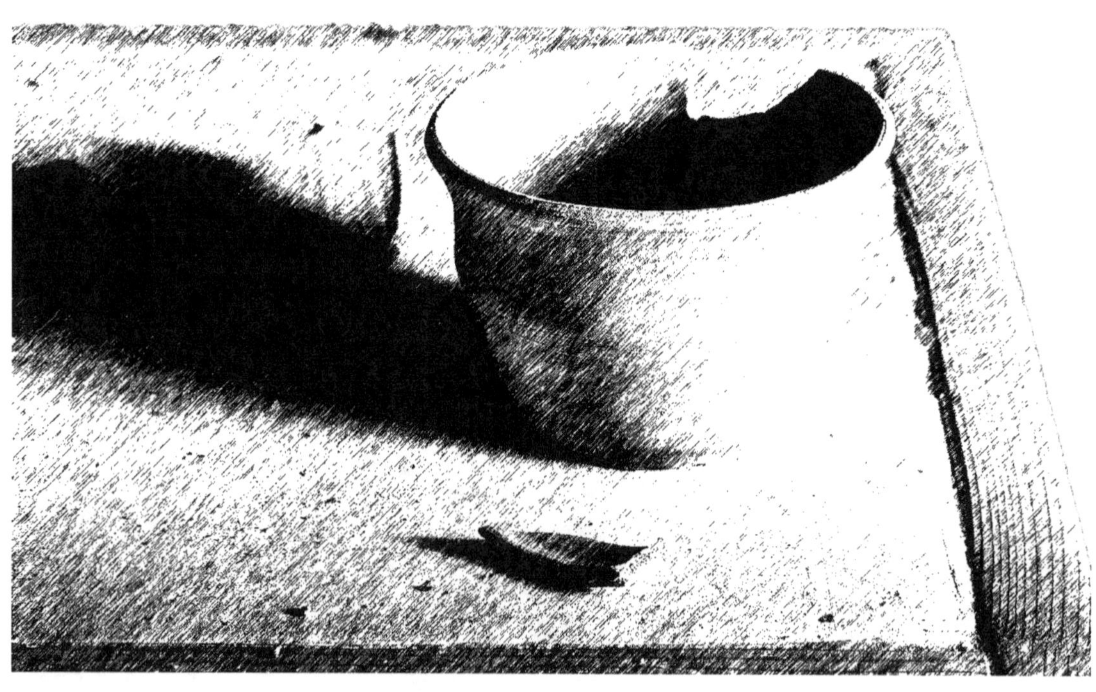

10

RENEWING

If the bone dry pot is chipped, cracked, or dropped, God is not daunted.

My Reading Notes:

One or two ideas in this chapter that I found new or surprising.

One or two questions that this chapter raised.

One or two places where this chapter spoke to me personally.

QUESTIONS FOR REFLECTION AND DISCUSSION:

1. Do you have broken pieces of some situation, some life dream, some relationship, some gift, or ability that seems broken beyond repair? Give the pieces to God in prayer—and see what he will do.

2. After my photographer broke that pot, he went to the potter and quickly apologized and offered to make restitution. She responded graciously, with strong words of forgiveness and encouragement. Is there something that you have broken but have not yet made right—a promise, a commitment, perhaps a possession? Even when we are careful, our words and actions can be destructive, and we need to do everything in our power to make things right. Are there things that you need to do this week to make amends?

AUTHOR'S PRAYER:

For this prayer time, let me pray this prayer over you:

Sovereign Lord, here, now, in the life of this precious one, there are disappointments and injuries of every kind. There are dreams that have died. There are people who have been lost. There are relationships broken. There are hopes dashed. There are longings that have remained unfulfilled.

O God, let these bones live. Restore, revive, refresh. Breathe on them, Breath of Life. Make them new. Amen.

MY PRAYER:

When you send your Spirit, they are created, and you renew the face of the ground. May the glory of the LORD endure forever; many the LORD rejoice in his works.
PSALM 104:30-31

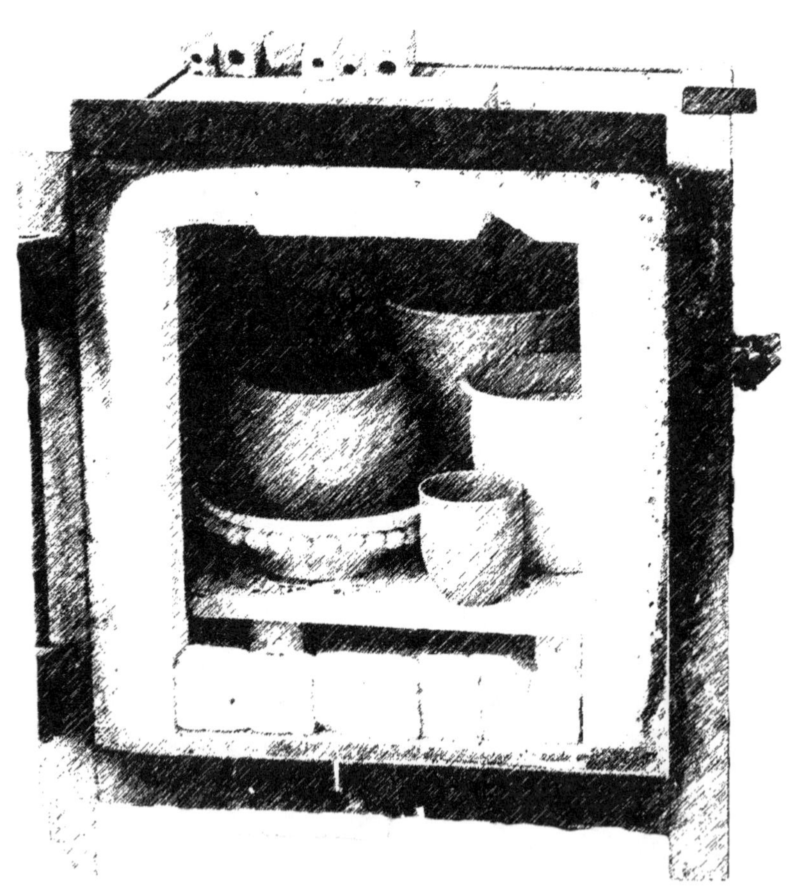

11 TRANSFORMING

The pot is gathered up, put into the kiln, and fired.

My Reading Notes:

One or two ideas in this chapter that I found new or surprising.

One or two questions that this chapter raised.

One or two places where this chapter spoke to me personally.

QUESTIONS FOR REFLECTION AND DISCUSSION:

1. What does it mean to you to be alert, ready for the return of the master and prepared for whatever trials may come? In what ways does your life reflect this readiness? In what ways might you adjust your day to better reflect this awareness?

2. Thank God for those who have stood by you during fiery trials. Then thank them: take time this week to write a note or make a call saying thank you to someone who has stood by you in tough times.

AUTHOR'S PRAYER:

Dear God. Consider my trials pure joy? Hmmm. I'm not there quite yet. But I'm learning, Lord, to accept good times and bad times as gifts from your hand. I'm learning to ask, "What is God saying to me in the midst of this circumstance?" And I'm starting to see that these things happen for a reason, that hardship can help to accomplish important things in my life, and that no matter how hot the fire gets, you mean it when you say that you will NEVER leave me, you will NEVER forsake me. I'm learning, Lord. Help me to learn it better. Help me to live it more. Amen.

MY PRAYER:

Now my soul is troubled, and what shall I say? "Father, save me from this hour?" No, it was for this very reason I came to this hour. Father, glorify your name.
JOHN 12:27-28

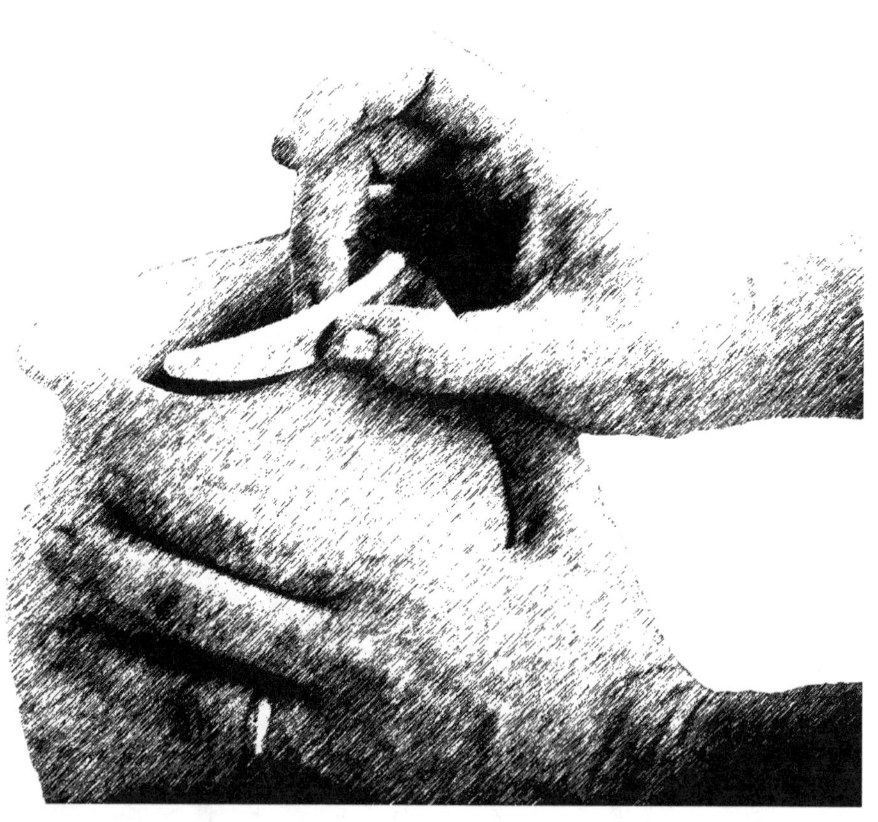

12 REPAIRING

If the fired pot is knocked over, cracked, dropped, or broken, God is not daunted.

My Reading Notes:

One or two ideas in this chapter that I found new or surprising.

One or two questions that this chapter raised.

One or two places where this chapter spoke to me personally.

QUESTIONS FOR REFLECTION AND DISCUSSION:

1. Is there a ministry you have now that is a result of hardship in your past? Or is there a ministry you might enter into now that builds upon the strength of your experiences for the benefit of others?

2. Are there worries, fears, needs, longings, injuries, or other treasures locked tight inside your heart, things that need to be broken open and poured out at the feet of Jesus? Do it in a way that you find meaningful: pray, worship, journal, talk, sing, create, walk, cry, dance, sew, paint, plant. Is this best addressed through time alone, through some activity, through words, or through personal time with a trusted friend or counselor or minister?

AUTHOR'S PRAYER:

Lord Jesus, everything in me wants to avoid the sacrifice of brokenness. But I'm beginning to see that much can be accomplished *because* of brokenness, not just in spite of it. Gideon's torches couldn't shine bright until the jars were shattered. Sweet anointing oil couldn't be spread on your feet until the box was crushed. And I know that the ultimate example is your own sacrifice, your body broken for me. Help me, Lord, to see how the pain and difficulty of my life can be a source of strength and healing for myself, and for others. Help me to understand the great mystery of Philippians 3:10, that the fellowship of your suffering leads to the power of your resurrection. Amen.

MY PRAYER:

My sacrifice, O God, is a broken spirit; a broken and contrite heart you, God, will not despise.
PSALM 51:17

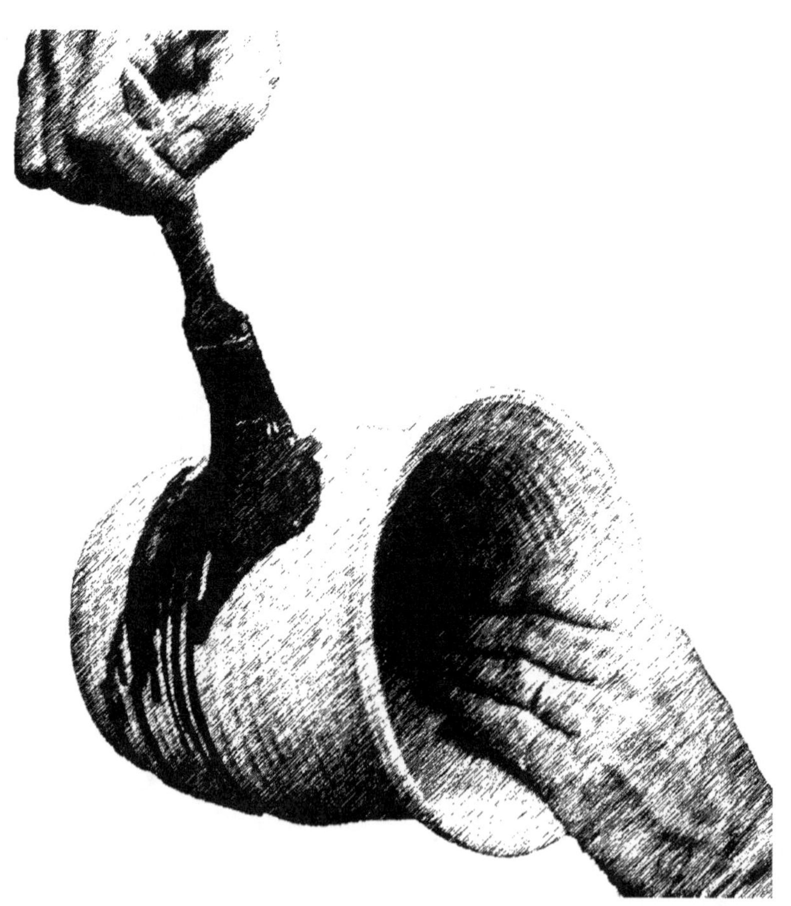

13 RETURNING

The pot is glazed and goes back into the fire.

My Reading Notes:

One or two ideas in this chapter that I found new or surprising.

One or two questions that this chapter raised.

One or two places where this chapter spoke to me personally.

QUESTIONS FOR REFLECTION AND DISCUSSION:

1. Is there some task that you have been afraid to face because you have been there before and it is too painful to imagine trying it again? Talk to God about it, and ask for the courage to persist in doing what is right.

2. Is there some ongoing task that has become very nearly unbearable, but still you sense the need to stay and faithfully complete it? Ask God to transform the mundane into the miraculous so that you can see his hand even in the midst of this circumstance.

AUTHOR'S PRAYER:

God, there are things in my life that are difficult because I really have counted the cost and experienced the pain and that makes it harder for me to persevere. I pray that you would either change my heart or change my circumstances. And whichever one you choose to do, I am determined to look for the ways that love, joy, peace, patience, kindness, goodness, faithfulness, gentleness, and self-control will abound in my life. Amen.

MY PRAYER:

But the fruit of the Spirit is love, joy, peace, forbearance, kindness, goodness, faithfulness, gentleness and self-control. Against such things there is no law.

GALATIANS 5:22-23

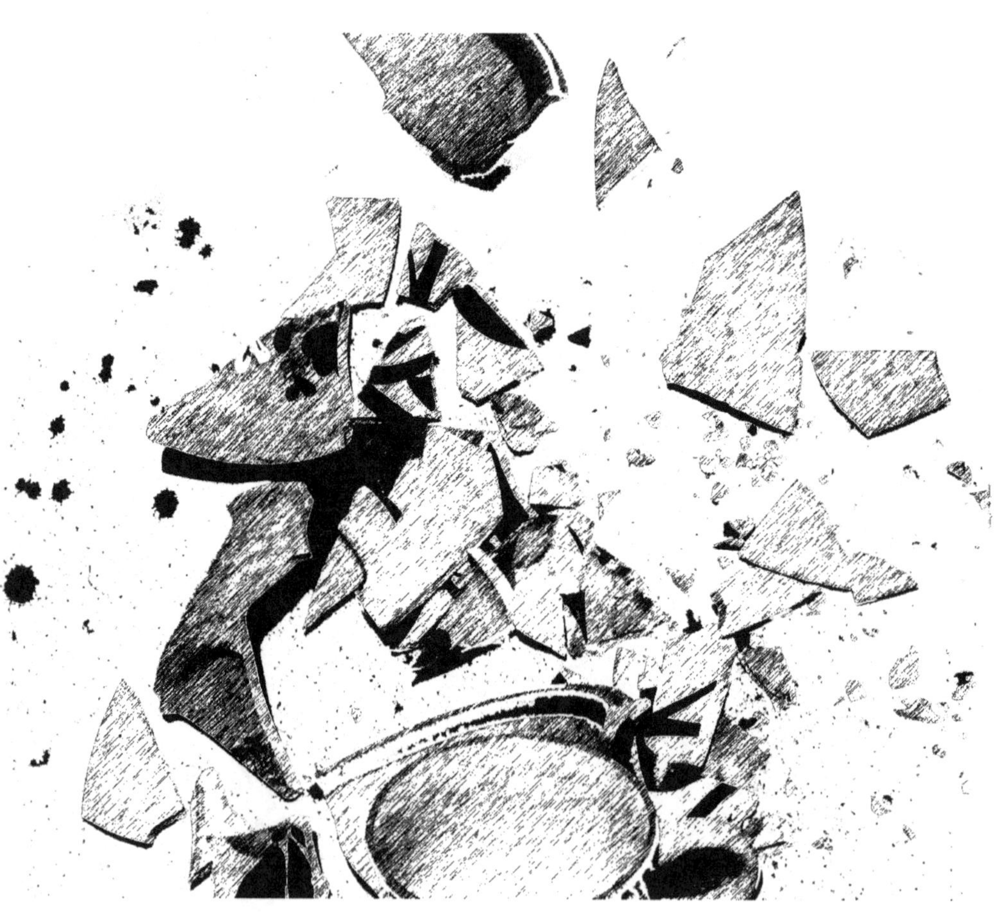

14
REDEEMING

If the finished pot is dropped and shattered, God is not daunted.

My Reading Notes:

One or two ideas in this chapter that I found new or surprising.

One or two questions that this chapter raised.

One or two places where this chapter spoke to me personally.

QUESTIONS FOR REFLECTION AND DISCUSSION:

1. List several situations where you have told yourself, "It's too late." Then offer the list to God in prayer.

2. Take time this week to appreciate the beauty of a mosaic, a quilt, a collage, a scrapbook page, or another art form that is made when an artist redeems bits and pieces by making something brand new. Or set aside time to use your own creative gifts in a new way.

AUTHOR'S PRAYER:

Change my heart, O God. Change my perspective. Help me to believe that you are able redeem the broken bits and pieces of my life. Even now. Help me to trust that you are ready and able to create something new. Amen.

MY PRAYER:

In your unfailing love you will lead the people you have redeemed. In your strength you will guide them to your holy dwelling.

EXODUS 15:13

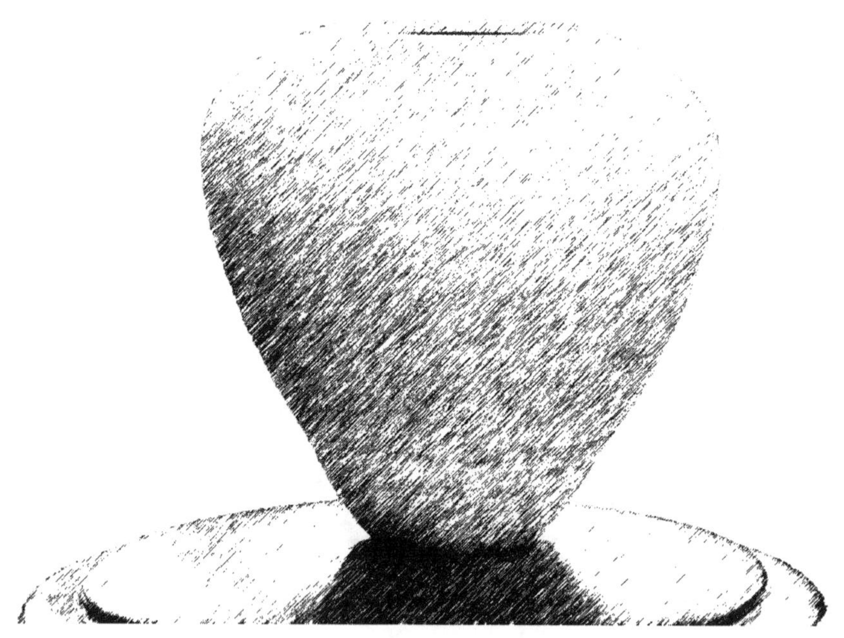

ABIDING 15

The pot is now strong and beautiful, ready for the Master's use.

My Reading Notes:

One or two ideas in this chapter that I found new or surprising.

One or two questions that this chapter raised.

One or two places where this chapter spoke to me personally.

QUESTIONS FOR REFLECTION AND DISCUSSION:

1. What step in the process do you most relate to in this season of your life?

2. Are there steps that you have been deliberately resisting, avoiding or neglecting? Ask God to make you willing to be made willing to surrender even to that process.

AUTHOR'S PRAYER:

God, I am fearfully and wonderfully made. You called me into being and have shaped me by your hand. Through the circumstances of my life, times of long dryness, times of intense fire, times of immeasurable blessing, you have been at work in many, mighty ways. Thank you that I am your workmanship. Now, Lord, help me to be faithful to the work you are calling me to do, today and every day, and throughout all the seasons of my life. Here I am. Made by the master. Here I am. Ready for your use. Amen.

MY PRAYER:

From the ends of the earth I call to you, I call as my heart grows faint; lead me to the rock that is higher than I. For you have been my refuge, a strong tower against the foe. I long to dwell in your tent forever and take refuge in the shelter of your wings.

PSALM 61:2-4

ACKNOWLEDGMENTS

I owe a great debt of thanks to many people who have encouraged and supported me, not only in this project but in the ongoing process of recognizing and cooperating with the hand of God in my daily life. In preparing this workbook, I would especially like to acknowledge the faithful collaboration of the Niños for persevering in faith and prayer; the Department of Art and Design at APU (especially Bill, Sue, Tom, Terry, and Guy) for encouraging my work; my father, James Sainsbury, for generous and unconditional support; Adam and Becky Bradley for the privilege of collaborating with their artistic vision; Carly Scholl for working with layout and scriptures; Barbara Hayes and Linda Spitser for eagle-eyed proofreading; and Lynn Maudlin for coming to the rescue (again and again).

And finally, my Sierra. You are a masterpiece of God's grace.

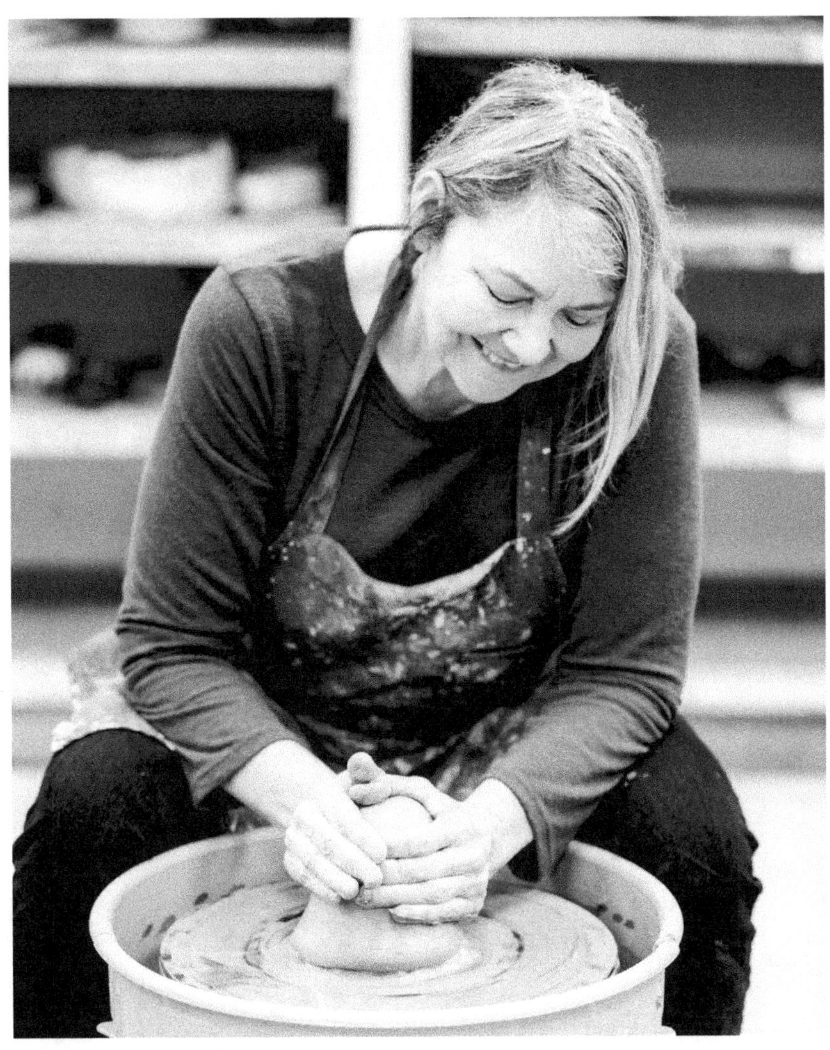

ABOUT THE AUTHOR

Diana Pavlac Glyer is a potter, a painter, and an avid gardener. She teaches in the Honors College at Azusa Pacific University. She enjoys the work of C.S. Lewis and J.R.R. Tolkien and has published books and articles about their creative process. She lives in southern California.

FOR MORE INFORMATION, VISIT HER ONLINE AT

WWW.DIANAGLYER.COM

Clay in the Potter's Hands WORKBOOK: SECOND EDITION
was designed and composed by
Matthew K. Tyler
in Arno Pro and Avenir
and published by

Lindale & Assoc.

A Division of TreeHouseStudios

www.ingramcontent.com/pod-product-compliance
Lightning Source LLC
LaVergne TN
LVHW080311110826
845155LV00023B/118

* 9 7 8 1 9 3 7 2 8 3 1 0 0 *